Makeup Tutorial for Beginners:

TRICKS AND TIPS HOW TO MAKE IDEAL MAKEUP

DESCRIPTION

Have you recently started using Make-up? Do you always feel a little overwhelmed by seeing its various products? If your answer is yes, then you need a complete Make-up guide that will answer all your questions and will simplify everything so that you can easily become a pro.

This ebook "Makeup tuotrial for beginners" has everything you need to know, including how to make an ideal Make-up box.

If you are a beginner, you may find lots of different ways to apply Make-up, like full-face coverage and a natural look. It can be hard for you to do Make-up if you have no idea which Make-up product to use. But in this book, you'll discover easy-to-follow Make-up methods. You'll find out valuable Make-up tricks and tips, and advice about Make-up removal to transform your look.

Following points have been discussed in this ebook:

- How to make an ideal make-up
- Kinds of make-up
- What accessories to use for Make-up and its removal
- When it is worth to do permanent Make-up
- How to care for the skin
- How to do Make-up removal correctly
- Top 7 make up tricks that always work
- Conclusion

Once you will buy this book, you will keep on checking this guide for quick tricks, guidance, and easy-to-follow instructions again and again. So what are you waiting for? Start your journey today!

TABLE OF CONTENTS

Tricks and Tips How to Make Ideal Makeup..1

Introduction   **1**

Chapter 1: How to make an ideal Make-up   **3**

Hide Dark Circles 3

Reassess and Perfect! 3

Make Me Pop... 4

Now Blush! 5

Add Some Definition 6

A Touch of Base 6

Get Lush Looking Lips 7

Chapter 2: Kinds of Make-up   **9**

HD Make-up.. 9

Matte Make-up.. 9

Airbrush Make-up 10

Mineral Make-up... 11

Shimmer Make-up 12

Normal Make-up 12

Smokey Make-up 13

Chapter 3: What accessories to use for make-up and make-up remover   16

Preliminary 16

Foundation 16

Pressed control/loose powder 16

Eyeliner 17

Highlighter 17

Defining eye shadow 17

Beauty blender 17

Mascara 17

Neutral eye shadow 18

Blush 18

Concealer 18

Translucent powder 18

Lipstick 18

Fluffy powder brush 19

Brush set 19

Eyeliner brush 19

Eye shadow brush 20

Tweezers 20

Setting a shower 20

Chapter 4: When it is worth to do permanent Make-up and what it is?   21

What it is 24

Chapter 5: How to care for the skin to make it look healthy   27

Eat a healthy diet.. 27

Protect yourself from the sun 28

    Seek shade 28

    Wear a protective dress..................... 28

    Use sunscreen..................................... 29

Treat your skin delicately............................. 29

    Shave cautiously................................. 29

    Pat dry 29

    Moisturize dry skin............................ 30

    Avoid strong cleansers 30

Limit bath time 30

Don't smoke 30

Manage stress 31

Chapter 6: How to do make-up removal correctly? 33

Pay Your Eye Area Extra Attention 33

Don't Miss Your Hairline 33

Clean Up with A Cotton Swab 34

Keep Make-up Remover Wipes by Your Bed 34

Use Toner After Cleansing 35

Follow Up with Moisturizer 35

Consider A Cleansing Oil 36

Chapter 7: Top 7 make up tricks that always work 37

Try powder lashes 37

Try to create A Conical shape for concealer. 38

Eye highlights 38

Do not ignore primer 39

Use Blush under Foundation 39

Apply a lip scrub before lipstick................... 39

Foundation should match your skin tone.... 40

Conclusion   **41**

INTRODUCTION

The art of Make-up has been rehashed and seen as an enhancer rather than as opposed to something that covers up. Different types of Make-up look move in the direction of achieving a similar objective upgrading the regular highlights and excellence of a person. Contrary to popular belief, Make-up isn't something that hides and changes how a person looks; in fact, different types of Make-up look are used to feature and highlight the genuine beauty of an individual.

With a shift in how ladies over the globe have made make up a part of their regular necessities, the cosmetic business has seen an all-time blast. New brands are turning out each day, promising better outcomes and making girls spoilt for decisions. There is a wide range of Make-up that works together to make the ideal Make-up look. But it's the Make-up as well as the style and system that issues.

You can be using similar items but different strategies to showcase different sorts of Make-up looks. Also, adapting some Make-up will help too. Presently, this might confuse us, but a Make-up artist can make a few sorts of Make-up looks, depending upon what you need, what results you want to accomplish, the event, and even the kind of skin type, tone, and personality you have.

Chapter 1: How to make an ideal Make-up

Hide Dark Circles

Apply a lotion with SPF to support concealer float on quickly.

Then use concealer just where you need it, like on under eye circles and flaws, choose a shade that ties your skin tone. Apply in slight stripes with a sharp concealer brush. At that point, mix using your ring finger for the lightest touch, and don't pull on fragile under-eye areas.

To get at fine lines, use the purpose of your brush.

Reassess and Perfect!

If a troublesome zit or imprint is as yet poking through, return and shroud it with an additional layer of concealer.

Use a similar kind as in stage one), or try concealment containing salicylic acid, like

Concealer, which helps psychologist flaws while disguising. Touch it onto issue areas with a pointed brush as opposed to slicking it on from the cylinder. Directly over the imperfection, but to avoid cakeyness, use your ring finger to pat its border outward until smooth.

For staying powder, apply powder over the top with a puff to adapt oil and keep concealed from sliding off late morning.

MAKE ME POP

Use bronze and gold cream shadows to provide eyes more profundity.

Apply the bronze shadow in your creases with a level shadow brush for more control, and use your fingers to smirch it down over the tops—avoid from the forehead bones. There shouldn't be any precise lines or stripes of color; it should look blended and smooth. To make everything move confirmation (significant with creamy formulas like these), set the cream with a similar powder eyeshadow or residue a drab translucent powder on top.

Then, to make eyes look much more significant, pat approximately gold cream shadow onto the focuses of your lids and run a slight along your lower lash lines with your finger or a small brush.

Using gold under eyes looks brilliant; darker shades can attract regard for under-eye circles.

Now Blush!

Leave concealing and chiseling cheekbones with a brush and powder, and try a cream blush instead for that shine from the inside outcome.

Relate to the apples of your cheeks, as observed here. Then blend the colors up toward your temples with your fingers or blush brush.

Gone overboard? Resolve a clown-like situation by applying a touch of foundation over the top instead of washing it all off and beginning from scratch

ADD SOME DEFINITION

For more intensity, edge your upper lash lines with a dark-colored liner pencil and smudge it upward with your shadow brush.

Then set with a similar powder eyeshadow used in the previous step. Completion off with two layers of mascara, like Smashbox Hyperlash Mascara, on top and base—concentrating on the external lashes with the top of the wand.

To give eyes a much higher lift, use an eyelash styler before you apply mascara. Start as near the underlying foundations of your lashes as possible and tenderly pulse the curler forward a small bit at a time to the surfaces.

A TOUCH OF BASE

To get superbly, even skin the fast way, use a foundation stick or liquid.

It's easy and gives you the exact bounty application. Draw solid lines down cheekbones, the sides of your nose, and above foreheads, and blend with your blender or Make-up brush. Want to look somewhat more sun-kissed? Before mixing, use a subsequent stick that is a few shades darker in all similar places for a sans streak sparkle (it looks dark in the photos, but we guarantee it melts directly in). Blend both colors over your face and down onto your neck using your fingers—the warmth from your hands will heat the foundation and help it glide.

Want lighter coverage? Rub the cream on your hands before you blend for a sheer, dewy completion.

GET LUSH LOOKING LIPS

Let it sink in well, and smear with a tissue if it feels oily. Using a strawberry-colors lipstick, straight from the tube, apply it to the focal point of your mouth (make a kissy face!), where shading will, in general, wear off first.

Blend the lipstick out over your lips, congratulating the colors on with at the tip of your finger to enable it to last. This gives you that fresh, just-ate-a-popsicle look. To amp up possessions for the night, contain a layer of sparkle for additional sparkle.

The path a bit of ice over your lips before slicking on sparkle to help color last all day and keep it from dying. Ta-da, you're finished!

Chapter 2: Kinds of Make-up

HD Make-up

HD, or High Definition, Make-up is the thing that we usually see people wearing on our TVs and the big screen. Accuracy cameras can easily catch every single line and crease on the face, both characteristic and framed by layers of Make-up. HD Make-up is a system that uses sheer Make-up that shrouds the lines and wrinkles and does not crease after some time. Hence, making the skin look faultless and camera-prepared for hours together.

The most beautiful part about HD Make-up is that it doesn't feel overwhelming and makes you look incredibly natural both on and off camera. It keeps your skin looking youthful and brilliant for a considerable length of time.

Matte Make-up

Matte Make-up is likely the most famous. It tends to be your natural look as well as made sensational for exceptional occasions. Matte

Make-up look allows you to try different things with bold colors and hues without removing the healthy look of your face. It's reliable and unobtrusive simultaneously and ideal for all weather types too.

It's an extraordinary Make-up look for all kinds of occasions and all seasons of the day. Its light allows your skin to inhale and looks striking. Matte Make-up arrives in a full scope of hues and tones, allowing numerous plausible outcomes to make staggering looks.

AIRBRUSH MAKE-UP

Airbrush Make-up is the canvas on Make-up with an airbrush instead of outdated Make-up application tools like brushes and wipes. It makes a layer of Make-up that has a smooth completion and makes you look flawless. It might feel somewhat overwhelming, especially if the climate is muggy, but it lasts for a considerable length of time.

Airbrush Make-up probably has the most perfect and smooth look of all the different kinds of Make-up looks. It covers any imperfections, dull spots, or composition differences without looking unnatural or cakey.

MINERAL MAKE-UP

Mineral Make-up uses chemical-free Make-up that doesn't harm the skin. Beautifying agents can be unforgiving and damage the skin, especially for individuals who have a touchy skin type. Mineral Make-up is regularly suggested by dermatologists and even skin pros after exceptional medicines are done to improve the skin. However, with the glowing for mineral Make-up, the decisions and potential outcomes are as much as some other kinds of Make-up looks.

Mineral Make-up causes no harm or damage to the skin. It uses compound-free Make-up beautifiers that are as beautiful as different sorts of Make-up look without settling on the skin's health.

Shimmer Make-up

Shimmer Make-up, as the name recommends, is all about shimmery and sparkly Make-up that makes you sparkle. It incorporates metallic shades and sparkle for the additional twinkle on the eyes. Shimmer Make-up procedures can be connected to all parts of the face, neck, shoulders, and neckline matters that remain to be worked out in your highlights. It makes a mystical touch to any clothing and occasion.

Shimmer Make-up can change one's look from easy to astounding. It's a pinch of additional radiance to make your sparkle and stand out. It's amazingly extraordinary for unique occasions that call for that sensational foot forward.

Normal Make-up

Not every person likes emotional, intense, and loud Make-up, especially for daytime looks and occasions. That is where the usual Make-up appearance comes in. It uses a light base to provide you an even tone, with unobtrusive hues to complement the highlights. It makes your debut 'all peaches and pinks,' only like you are becoming flushed.

It's the flawless Make-up look when you want to look extraordinary but not all made-up. It has the advantage of making you look faultless while not diverting from your obvious highlights.

SMOKEY MAKE-UP

Smokey Make-up works at making an incredibly hot look with dim eyes and intense lips. The principal focal point of this style of Make-up is the eyes. Shades of blacks and dark are used to make a dark Smokey look, and shades of brown may be used to create a delicate Smokey look. Long phony lashes, Kohl, and an eyeliner complete the eyes. Depending on the occasion, time, and day, the Make-up artist may use an intense lip color or even leave them bare just to feature the eyes.

Smokey Make-up is about the modern lady who is equal parts active and incredible. It has an incredibly sexy intrigue, without looking too present-day or even varied.

With such a significant number of different sorts of Make-up looks, it can be tough to tell what's best for you, especially on a day as extraordinary as your wedding. You want to look impeccable but not break the entire look because of the wrong Make-up look. Here are a few clues to allow you to pick the right sort of Make-up looks for different wedding services:

➢ Permanently take a trial session much before the big day.

➢ Choose different sorts of Make-up looks for different occasions, depending upon the climate, wedding outfit, lighting, and time of the event.

➢ Pamper your skin, exercising, and healthy skin system for at any rate two months before the wedding for an expected glow and better Make-up results.

➢ Talk to a specialized Make-up artist to better cognize what works with your skin type.

Chapter 3: What accessories to use for make-up and make-up remover

These basics ought to be the formation of your beauty arsenal. Consider this a definitive everyday Make-up kit.

Preliminary

It's the most essential to set your foundation and other Make-up correctly.

Foundation

All over your face, you don't want to slather it—just in spots where you see uneven skin tone or staining. If you don't need as much inclusion as foundation gives, consider a tinted moisturizer instead.

Pressed control/loose powder

Pressed powder or loose powder is for to give you a flawless finish after foundation and concealer.

EYELINER

You can custom your darker shade of eye shadow as a liner along the lashes—or use a dark brown or colored pencil to make a thin line that will define and improve your eyes.

HIGHLIGHTER

Highlighter gives you a glow complete that enhances your Make-up to the next level.

DEFINING EYE SHADOW

Choose a medium, impartial shade like a warm brown or charcoal dark. Brush it in the crinkle of the eye, under the brow bone, to add depth.

BEAUTY BLENDER

It's an unquestionable requirement need unit for your Make-up. It's used in blending your foundation and concealer.

MASCARA

There's no better method to define your eyes than by raising your lashes. Stick with basic dark (or dull darker if you have light hair and lashes).

NEUTRAL EYE SHADOW

An impartial beige or beige is a moment brightener when swiped all over the cover.

BLUSH

Appearance for a warm tone to add a pop of colors to the apples of your cheeks.

CONCEALER

Choose a creamy formula that can stow away under-eye circles and cover imperfections.

TRANSLUCENT POWDER

A snappy, light cleaning of powder sets Make-up and controls sparkle.

LIPSTICK

How about some colors? Lipstick (or shine, if you want a progressively casual look) is the ideal antidote to the funk.

Fluffy Powder Brush

Have one major, rounded brush to neat on powder once you've completed your Make-up.

Brush set

You should need a different kind of brush set to characterizing your face as well as your eyes. As like:

- Contour brush
- Foundation brush
- Highlight brush
- Blush brush

This brush is somewhat smaller than your powder brush and is the correct size for spotting the cheeks and blending along the cheekbones.

Eyeliner brush

A small, level, the angled brush can be used to line the eyes or include a touch of temples powder to thin eyebrows.

EYE SHADOW BRUSH

An all-over brush that gets your top shrouded.

TWEEZERS

Clean up any stray hairs around your foreheads that grow up in between temples arrangements.

SETTING A SHOWER

After all, Make-up did you need to spray setting spray with the goal that you can keep your Make-up last longer.

CHAPTER 4: WHEN IT IS WORTH TO DO PERMANENT MAKE-UP AND WHAT IT IS?

It's hard enough to set yourself up each morning, but things get ugly once you understand the total number of things you need to juggle in your hands. From preparing your children for school to preparing up for a stressful day at work, you are, without a doubt, vigilant for anything that can spare you even a couple of valuable minutes. This is actually what lasting Make-up can achieve for you. In the midst of all the free for in your morning schedule, you have one less thing to stress over by jumping on this pattern.

The term permanent Make-up may mood killer to a few people, but this pattern has been developing in ubiquity in the progression of recent years. The procedure is regularly contrasted with getting a tattoo, as it includes applying colors to the top layer of the skin. Calling it permanent can be viewed as a contradiction because the Make-up tends to fade over time. You need to visit a perpetual Make-up artist now and then for contact-ups.

It's easy to see the practical advantages of getting lasting Make-up, but it also establishes valuable for masking tasteful issues, for example, alopecia, vitiligo, and scars. And what's incredible is that you can figure out how to apply permanent Make-up yourself by joining up with an online course. Exclusive Brows, for example, offers key and propelled master classes for both manual and machine permanent Make-up.

You can just contact a qualified professional to enable you to achieve the look you want. During the underlying interview, hope to be asked relevant inquiries concerning what kind of Make-up you plan on getting. The application procedure typically takes an hour or two, depending upon the region to be dealt with. Note that the colors may seem darker just after the treatment, but it soon fades to your favored shade. Different variables impact the rate at which the Make-up fades, but the most widely recognized culprit is over-the-top sun introduction.

The application of lasting beautifying cosmetics is usually made on the eyebrows, eyelids, lips, and cheeks. While you shouldn't hope to show signs of improvement results than manual application, understand that you're mostly paying for comfort. Some may dislike the idea of looking all fab even when precisely at home, while others appreciate each moment they get the opportunity to spare.

Moving forward means you get the chance to appreciate to enjoy hands glamming up. However, you may need to return to your specialist for contact-ups to guarantee your Make-up always looks incredible. Also, it pays to go for a timeless look, so you can sit back and relax, realizing that your Make-up won't look dated after only a couple of years.

Just like getting tattoos, there's a degree of risk involved in enduring Make-up application.

You can experience the ill effects of skin responses or secure certain wellbeing conditions. This is the reason you must select a technician carefully. Don't take shortcuts, as you will want to take care of business right the first run-through. Point of confinement your decisions to specialists who convey the proper license and use sterile hardware to limit the danger of contamination.

What it is

Permanent Make-up, also recognized as micro-pigmentation, cosmetic tattooing, and Intradermal Pigmentation, is a radical cosmetic technique that includes the use of a pen covering iron oxide to have a permanent pigmentation of the dermis. It is realized by implanting natural colored pigments into the dermal layer of the skin. The way uses an excellent needle that makes hundreds of tiny perforations per minute. It produces articulate designs that resemble Make-up which is usually done on lips, eyelids, and eyebrows.

Permanent Make-up, also identified as cosmetic tattooing, micro-pigmentation, and Intradermal Pigmentation, is a revolutionary cosmetic technique that includes the use of a pen containing iron oxide to have a perpetual pigmentation of the dermis. It is accomplished by embedding common shaded colors into the dermal layer of the skin. The system uses an excellent needle that makes many little punctures every moment. It produces understandable plans that resemble Make-up which is generally done on lips, eyelids, and eyebrows.

Every strategy takes between 30 to 120 minutes relying upon its unpredictability. Qualified technicians use an analgesic to numb the region being tattooed. At first, the color will seem more brilliant or darker, but after some time, it will blur. The zone will be swollen inside 2-5 days, and the outside layer will frame before mending, simply like a typical tattoo.

Permanent Make-up has been regularly used as a cosmetic enhancement, and it's used as concealment for stretch imprints, pigmentations, age spots, and uneven stains. The technique helps individuals who are enduring ailments like alopecia, vitiligo, and people who experienced chemotherapy.

Chapter 5: How to care for the skin to make it look healthy

Good skincare — plus sun protection and gentle scrubbing — can keep your skin healthy and glowing.

You can, in any situation, treat yourself by acing the basics. Great healthy skin and healthy lifestyle decisions can help defer normal maturing and anticipate different skin issues. Begin with these five simple tips.

Eat a healthy diet

A healthy diet can enable you to look and feel your best. Eat a lot of fruits, vegetables, entire grains, and lean proteins. The association between diet and skin break out isn't clear — but some exploration suggests that a monotonous eating wealthy in fish oil or fish oil enhancements and low in unhealthy fats and handled or refined honey may improve more youthful observing skin. Drinking a lot of water supports to keep your skin hydrated.

Protect yourself from the sun

One of the most significant tactics to deal with your skin is to the protection it from the sun. A period of sun overview can cause wrinkles, age spots, and other skin issues — as well as increase the danger of skin cancer.

For complete sun security:

Seek shade

Escape the sun between 10 a.m. and 4 p.m., when the sun's beams are most grounded.

Wear a protective dress

Spread your skin with firmly woven long-sleeved shirts, long jeans, and wide-overflowed caps. Also, think about clothing added substances, which give attire an extra layer of ultraviolet protection for a specific number of washings, or uncommon sun-defensive dress specifically intended to square bright beams.

USE SUNSCREEN

Use a wide range of sunblock with an SPF of in some events 15. Put on sunscreen liberally, and reapply at consistent intervals — or more frequently if you're swimming or sweating.

TREAT YOUR SKIN DELICATELY

Daily cleansing and shaving can negatively affect your skin. To keep it delicate:

SHAVE CAUTIOUSLY

To secure and lubricate your skin, apply shaving cream, salve, or gel before shaving. For the nearest shave, use a perfect, sharp razor. Shave toward the direction the hair develops, not against it.

PAT DRY

After washing or bathing, gently pat or blotch your skin dry with a towel, so some dampness stays.

MOISTURIZE DRY SKIN

If your skin is dry, practice a moisturizer that accommodates your skin type. For everyday use, consider a moisturizer that contains SPF.

AVOID STRONG CLEANSERS

Solid cleansers and cleansers can band oil from your skin. Instead, pick mellow chemicals.

LIMIT BATH TIME

Warm water and lengthy showers or baths remove oils from your skin. Farthest point your shower or shower time, and use warm — instead of hot — water.

DON'T SMOKE

Smoking creates your skin aspect more seasoned and contributes to wrinkles. Smoking strait the minor veins in the outer layers of skin, which decreases bloodstream and makes skin paler. This also drains the skin of oxygen and supplements that are imperative to skin health.

Smoking also harms collagen and elastin — the filaments that give your skin quality and elasticity. Moreover, the dreary outward appearances you make when smoking —, for example, tightening your lips when living in and squinting your eyes to keep out smoke— can contribute to wrinkles.

Also, smoking increases your danger of squamous cell skin cancer. If you smoke, the ideal approach to ensure your skin is to stop. Ask your doctor for tips or medicines to enable you to quit smoking.

MANAGE STRESS

Uncontrolled stress can make your skin progressively delicate and trigger skin inflammation breakouts and other skin issues. To support healthy skin — and a healthy state of mind — take steps to deal with your stress. Get enough sleep, set reasonable cutoff points, rationalize your plan for the day, and set aside a few minutes to do the things you appreciate.

The outcomes may be more emotional than you anticipate.

Chapter 6: How to do make-up removal correctly?

Pay Your Eye Area Extra Attention

Eye Make-up can be famously difficult to remove, which is why there are so many Make-up removers implied explicitly for removing those troublesome (as far as expulsion just) fluid eyeliners and durable mascaras. If your standard removal doesn't cut it, attempt one that is about the eyes. Gently sweep a cotton cushion drenched with the remover over your shut covers and ta-da, instant removal.

Don't Miss Your Hairline

If you worked admirably applying your foundation, it ought to go all the path to your hairline. In this way, remember to expel your Make-up from that region, too! You may get your underlying foundations somewhat wet, contingent upon your remover of decision, but it's well accepted, despite all the trouble to be perfect.

CLEAN UP WITH A COTTON SWAB

Sometimes, no matter how hard you attempt, there is, by all accounts, a smidgen of Make-up left in difficult to arrive at areas. A minor piece of foundation around your nose or a smear of eyeliner against your lash line. The secret to disposing of even those most challenging Make-up remnants is to use a cotton swab to get specific with your evacuation. Plunge a swab in Make-up remover and remove exactly what you want to see vanish.

KEEP MAKE-UP REMOVER WIPES BY YOUR BED

A couple of simple swipes of a Make-up remover wipe can clean skin of foundation, concealer, and eye shadow. Furthermore, you get the fulfillment of seeing what has fallen off of your face on the wipe. Search for choices that are without alcohol so your skin doesn't feel dry post-use. Begin by cleaning your face free of Make-up and follow up by purging your appearance and tapping dry. Make-up wipes are perfect if you now and then battle to finish your healthy skin routine during the evening. Preserve a pack on your nightstand; that way, you can rapidly get clean even if you refuse to get up.

Use Toner After Cleansing

Toner can be used as an additional purifying advance after using your wash-off facial cleanser. It just pauses for a moment, and it might help clear away the remaining parts of heavy Make-up. Just soak a cotton cushion with a couple of drops and delicately wipe it over your skin. Try choices that are non-drying to help ensure against moisture loss.

Follow Up with Moisturizer

Whichever Make-up and purifying arrangements you use, it's critical to apply moisturizer afterward. Try not to get dry before finishing this progression since it's best to apply moisturizer directly to the skin while it's sodden, as this can help lock in more hydration.

CONSIDER A CLEANSING OIL

Purging oils are an excellent alternative if you wear heavy eye Make-up or have dry skin since purifying oil can help evacuate obstinate eyeliner and mascara without any scouring or pulling. Apply a couple of beads to a cotton cushion and spot it over your skin.

Purifying oil can be supportive and less brutal on dry skin—especially the sensitive skin around your eyes. Purifying oils are well-known picks for twofold purging, and that is actually what you'll want to do if you use one. After purging with your oil, make sure to catch up with another facial cleanser after, so your skin doesn't turn out to be extra slick looking as you sleep.

Chapter 7: Top 7 make up tricks that always work

Do you know that you will need to understand a lot of things if you want to have a flawless Make-up look? Make-up is an art and complete skill, from nailing to the right product order for getting a beautiful look. To achieve the flawless look that everyone admires, all you need is a positive attitude, consistent effort, and a few tricks that you should learn.

Here are few of them that you can learn easily.

Try powder lashes

Have you ever tried to notice what the secret to longer lashes is? A small quantity of transparent powder. All you need to do is dust your lashes with a light application of loose powder after your initial coat of mascara to give them more volume and make them appear longer. Interesting trick, right?

TRY TO CREATE A CONICAL SHAPE FOR CONCEALER.

Most people are used to applying concealer in a semi-circular pattern, especially under the eyes area, to hide any sign of puffiness. But if you will apply the concealer in a conical pattern under the eyes and to the end of your nose, you will get the best results. It will not only conceal better due to its application, but it also aids in the contouring of the sides of your nose.

EYE HIGHLIGHTS

When it comes to the question of creating a naturally stunning eye Make-up look, the placement of highlights correctly is very important. Lighter shades (whites, creams, and pearls) should be used on the inner corners, the middle of the eye, and just behind the brow bone. You can start with the light colors and then use darker shades and properly mix them for better results.

Do not ignore primer

When it comes to a question about your skin preparation, you should choose Make-up primer. Make-up primer is a fantastic option available in the market for creating a smooth look for your Make-up. It will also help your Make-up last for a long time, and you will use it before applying foundation to your skin.

Use Blush under Foundation

This is one of the best tricks to attain the best results. All you need to do is reverse the sequence in which you apply the blush on and foundation. You will apply the blush first, then the foundation on top of that. The final look will give the impression that you are gleaming, and it will give a natural look.

Apply a lip scrub before lipstick

A beautiful pout always gives a ravishing final touch to any Make-up look. So, I think it will be a good idea to start with a smooth base to keep your lips in top shape. This process can help you in getting rid of dead skin cells that have accumulated on the surface of your lips. Just give your lips a gentle scrub before applying your lipstick with the touch of your finger. It is done!

FOUNDATION SHOULD MATCH YOUR SKIN TONE

With so many foundation options and colors to select from, it is natural to feel puzzled. You would want to select one that matches your skin tone. That involves finding the right foundation. For Instance, if you have a dry skin, you can use Infallible Pro-Glow Foundation to moisturize it. Or, if your skin is oily, you can use another option. So take this decision carefully. Always make sure to apply your foundation in dabbing motions for better results.

CONCLUSION

Make-up is a fun activity. And having the proper Make-up at the right time might make you feel confident about yourself. When it comes to the latest trend of Make-up, like what works and what is merely hype in the Make-up industry, media and marketing provide great insight.

However, if you are a passionate beginner in the world of Make-up, it may appear to be hard for you to do Make-up at the start. It requires mastering lots of steps, including a selection of your Make-up supplies, tools, and brushes, as well as working out the best application techniques. But, to overcome this "major problem," I know that having a few secrets, tips, and hacks in one's place can be extremely beneficial for Make-up beginners.

As a Make-up student first thing to consider is skin preparation, even if you are only planning to have light Make-up. A pre-Make-up routine is nothing more than your daily cleanse-tone-moisturize routine, which washes and hydrates your face to ensure that Make-up lies properly and evenly on your skin so you can have a smooth look.

Secondly, knowing your skin type is also essential if you want Make-up that looks beautiful, lasts all day, and doesn't cause any pimples. You will get Make-up products in a variety of formulas (creams, liquids, powders, etc.). Knowing your skin type will determine which type of product is best for you and your skin. So, before you buy anything for your collection, the first thing you need to do is to learn about your skin type.

So whether it's for a regular day or a special occasion, such as a wedding, a business meeting, or a date, we all want to look our best or beautiful. Therefore it is very important that one must have a comprehensive resource. This ebook will serve this purpose.

It will guide you on how to have flawless glamour Make-up, how to create amazing eyes look with eye shadow, eyeliner, and mascara, how to remove Make-up by using simple products, and which color to use on your lips to pull the look together. It also contains information about what things you must follow in order to keep your skin fresh and what is about different types of Make-up looks like.

If you're ready to dive into the world of beauty or want to learn how to improve your Make-up skills, you've come to the right place. Buy this ebook today to become a pro and to face the world like a superstar!

Printed in Great Britain
by Amazon

24224939R00030